Leadership is the greatest challenge and opportu[nity...]
The good news is that Leadership isn't some mys[tery...]
the preserve of a few. It's a mindset, a set of pract[ices...]
learn, practice and evolve for ourselves. That's th[e...]

"A good leadership book", unpacking and demystifying great leadership. It's brilliantly accessible, deeply respectful of the reader and packed with insight and wisdom that you can apply, immediately.

— Carl Sanders-Edwards, Founder and CEO, Adeption

This is an insightful book on what it takes to be a leader in the modern world. It is full of tools, tips and strategies that will help both the new and experienced leader. The bite size sections make it easy to read for the leader on the go. Digest and apply.

— Nick Petrie, Co-Founder, Vertical Mindset Indicator

Reading A Good Leadership Book, I thought of the Mark Twain quote: "I didn't have time to write a short letter, so I wrote a long one instead." This is no Twain letter! Instead, Dan has packed a thousand pages of wisdom into an engaging, fast-paced, and provocative guide that's a mere fraction of that length.
Highly recommended!

— Jeff Grimshaw, partner, MGStrategy; Author of *Five Frequencies* and *Leadership without Excuses*

I've known Dan Lake for more than a decade, closer to two. One word summarizes him: character. Chapter 8 on "Question Best Practice" makes this whole book worth it.

— Ron Smith Th.D, Co-Founder, SBS International; Author of *Read to Lead*

This book helps any leader understand how important it is that they help bring Clarity in key areas, which helps shape Culture and how great Communication is critical for this. Read, reflect, learn and enjoy.

— Mark Powell, Independent Director; former-CEO, The Warehouse Group

Dan Lake has the gift of taking complex theories and breaking them down into easy to understand concepts. By using The Motivation Tree, Dan gave me clarity on how to help Millennials take action with their financial goals. The book is an enjoyable read that almost feels like a conversation but you come away with skills that are easy to put into action.

— Linda Sturgess, Head of Private Capital, Bank of New Zealand

A Good Leadership Book simplifies ideas so you can approach them one step at a time, brings them to life through memorable stories, provokes thinking and promotes the reader to take action. I recommend it as a must-read for every leader!

— Mark Watkins, VP of Sales & Delivery, JumpShift Development

A GOOD LEADERSHIP BOOK

On Clarity, Culture & Communication

DAN LAKE

First published 2023

Published by Lead Coach Release Ltd

www.leadcoachrelease.com

Copyright © Dan Lake, 2023

The moral rights of the author have been asserted.

All rights reserved. No part of this publication may be reproduced, stored in a retrieval system, or transmitted in any form or by any means without the prior permission of the copyright owner.

A catalogue record for this book is available from the National Library of New Zealand.

Paperback ISBN: 978-0-473-66197-7

Ebook ISBN: 978-0-473-66199-1

Every effort has been made to contact copyright holders. However, the publisher will happily remedy in subsequent editions any inadvertent omissions brought to their attention.

To the maximum extent permitted by law the publisher and author exclude all liability for any errors or omissions, and for any loss, damage or expense (whether direct or indirect) suffered by a third party relying on information contained in this book.

Cover & Design by DJL

Typeset in EB Garamond and Montserrat

Heather - Thank you & I love you
This is the final version. I promise.

To my girls
This book is for you.

And to the aspiring leaders
May you have wisdom on the road.

CONTENTS

INTRODUCTION	**vii**
PART ONE: CLARITY	**01**
PART TWO: CULTURE	**67**
PART THREE: COMMUNICATION	**137**
WHERE TO FROM HERE?	**208**
MUST READ BOOKS	**210**
ABOUT THE AUTHOR	**213**

01

PART ONE: CLARITY

03	RESISTANCE IS A SIGN OF ENGAGEMENT
09	CLARITY
15	HOW CAN I HELP YOU SUCCEED?
21	IT'S NOT MY RANCH
27	IMPLICATIONAL THINKING
33	LEADERSHIP SHADOW
41	THE MOTIVATION TREE
49	QUESTION BEST PRACTICE
53	AUTHORITY RESPONSIBILITY
59	DON'T BUILD A CRISIS

02

PART TWO: CULTURE

CELEBRITY VS. SERVICE	**69**
2 CULTURES	**75**
BLAME	**81**
PRETENDING IS PRACTICING	**89**
URGE	**95**
THE LEADERSHIP FOOD PYRAMID	**99**
HOW TO BE A TOXIC BOSS	**111**
WHAT DOES THIS CHANGE MEAN FOR ME?	**119**
THE GOLDEN GOOSE OF MANAGEMENT	**125**
PERSONAL VALUES LIFE CYCLE	**129**

03

PART THREE: COMMUNICATION

139	THE 1 FT FENCE
145	INTENT VS. IMPACT
151	MICROFEEDBACK
155	SMOKE, FLAGS, & ROCKETS
163	REFRAME FLEXIBILITY: POSSIBILITY
169	HIDDEN MEANINGS
177	WHAT MIGHT BE POSSIBLE IF?
185	FOUR HURDLES OF DELEGATION
193	PRESPOND
199	CONNECT BEYOND VISION

INTRODUCTION

▶ When I was a kid, I flew with my Dad to a remote part of Fiordland National Park in New Zealand. My Dad is a carpenter. He was building a back-country hut—nothing fancy; a stone fireplace, a few bunks, metal sides, a roof, and a porch. If you've ever hiked anywhere in New Zealand, you know the type I mean.

When the helicopter landed, we off-loaded our gear. A few simple hand tools. A saw. A hammer. Tape measures and nails. Nothing fancy. Nothing electric. Simple tools.

This book is about giving simple tools for good leadership. Use what works for you right now.

Consider going through one chapter a day – or a week – giving time to reflect on the takeaways and implement the challenges at the end of each chapter. Adapt it for your own leadership practice. Adopt it with your team – talk about what mini actions or changes you might make together.

It is simple. Pick it up. Put it down. Leave it on the coffee table until you need a little inspiration. Then pick it up again and try something new.

But whatever you do: Lead. Lead well. Lead wisely. Step up and have a go. The world needs great leaders. The world needs you.

—— **PART ONE** ——

01
CHAPTER

> **WHAT IS OUR RESPONSE TO QUESTIONS OR RESISTANCE?**

RESISTANCE IS A SIGN OF ENGAGEMENT

▶ At a leadership conference in Vancouver, BC, a participant asked me the following questions; "How do we get our employees to work with the systems and processes we have in place? And how do we get them to stop trying to change all our systems?"

I replied, "Why should they? Why should people care about the processes your organization currently utilizes? Why should they stop trying to bring change? Why should any employee stop?"

My answer was not disrespectful. Questions and challenge are an opportunity to look and see if a system or process is, in fact, no longer necessary.

For leaders, employees' actions to completely reshape systems and processes feel like resistance. Some leaders believe any resistance shows team members don't want to participate. That they're not on board, that there is no buy-in.

This couldn't be further from the truth.

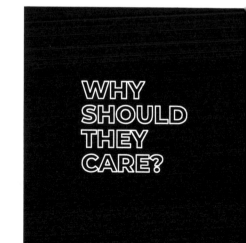

Teams want to bring change, protest existing systems, and question organizational dynamics because they deeply care about the success of their work. Resistance is not a negative trait to be stamped out. Resistance is a positive trait that shows engagement with issues, ideas, and tasks.

Resistance proves employees are engaged within an organization or a team. Disengaged staff will not speak up; they will not resist or protest. They simply won't care.

Protest against seemingly (to them) unnecessary constraints is a sign of engagement. It is a sign an employee wants to succeed.

Consider this: Do people resist a system or structure because they are protecting something else? What might that be? And why might it be important to your team?

For example, maybe they are protecting their well-being at work.

It could be that the current system of working in cubicles rather than an open plan environment is a challenge for them.

Or maybe your team is from a majority group culture instead of an individualistic culture. Maybe well-being looks like being visible and present with one another at mealtimes and breaks.

They deeply care about the success of the work they do

If you're facing resistance, ask yourself, "How does this resistance show engagement?"

And then ask, "How can we engage together to see our organization succeed?"

TAKEOUT

When a team member pushes back, consider what they are protecting or trying to engage with. Look at systems, values, and ways of working as starting points for reviewing how resistance is a sign of engagement.

CHALLENGE

Write out the last challenging question(s) you were asked as a leader. Try exploring the resistance further. Ask more questions. Listen deeply. Believe people care about something - so find out what it is.

02
CHAPTER

> **WHAT DO YOU NEED TO UNDERSTAND TODAY TO HAVE CLARITY? PURPOSE, POSITION, OR PRIORITIES?**

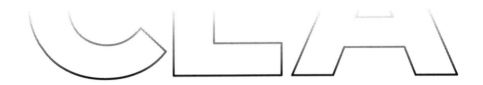

▶ Clarity of Purpose

Purpose is overarching. It is the 10,000 ft view. What is your goal? What are you trying to do? What gets you up in the morning?

At another level: How is your next meeting supposed to help achieve your goals for the week or month or year? How does your last purchase order promote long-term outputs and sustainable business?

One of the most significant leadership challenges is clearly defining purpose. It's much easier to get stuck into the day-to-day, into the to-done lists, and a plethora of details.

Great leaders define the organization's purpose (or meeting or sub-group) and engage in the hard work of keeping that clear purpose in front of the team.

What is your purpose?

Clarity of Position

The TV mini-series Band of Brothers follows a group of men during World War Two working their way across Europe as the spearhead of the Allied invasion to retake the continent.

Repeatedly, officers and men stop to gather around a map to determine their position. It doesn't matter if it's raining, or if bombs are falling, or if it is breakfast time - the map comes out.

They were asking, "Where are we?"

Clarity of Position is about an accurate assessment of what is around us. It's about where we are.

Can we clearly articulate where we are in comparison to our competitors? Relative to our short, medium, and long-term goals? Against the broader economy and the winds of change within society?

Where are we?

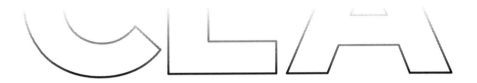

Clarity of Priorities

Have you ever seen the illustration about time management and trying to get everything (rocks, stones, sand) inside a glass jar?

It turns out, if you place in all the big rocks first, there is room for the stones, and finally, the sand to pack around it all. It does all fit, but only if you start with the big rocks.

Think about your priorities: "What is most important right now, and how do you know?"

Distractions will come into the week. Emergencies will seem to overwhelm our systems and structures. Therefore, it is essential to keep a good eye on priorities and communicate those priorities to our team.

What is most important? And how clearly does your team know?

KITTY

How would you describe what you do to a five-year-old?

TAKEOUT

To have clarity, leaders must regularly ask three key questions.
1. What is our purpose?
2. Where are we in relation to that purpose?
3. What is most important right now?

CHALLENGE

Get a sticky note - Answer the three questions above for your role or your organization in no more than three sentences.

Based on your answers, what do you notice about the clarity you have (or need)?

03
CHAPTER

WHAT IS THE MOST IMPORTANT QUESTION YOU CAN ASK AS A LEADER?

HOW CAN I HELP YOU SUCCEED?

▶ Whether you're the CEO, CFO, chairman of the board, or the newbie in the office running to get coffee – it doesn't matter – these six words change everything.

How can I help you succeed?

Outstanding leadership is built on answering this question.

Look at Jeff Bezos: He asked, "How can I help you succeed?" in getting books to your home faster. Now you can get almost anything to your home faster through Amazon. Jeff helps people succeed at shopping.

I have a friend who started a non-profit architecture firm. They help people in places like Nepal, Mexico, and Cambodia successfully construct sustainable buildings.

They invest in helping communities succeed. They show outstanding leadership by helping others succeed.

At every level, of every organization, and every day, we need to all ask, "How can I help you succeed?"
What do you need?
What frustrates you?
What can I do to help move your project along a little further?

To help someone succeed, maybe try asking, "What's hindering you from the next step, and how can we overcome that obstacle?"

Imagine if everyone in your company asked, "How can I help you succeed" every day? How would it alter teamwork, efficiency, and morale?

Success starts with you. Today, ask, "How can I help you succeed?"

They are the best six words you'll ever learn.

HOW CAN I HELP YOU SUCCEED?

TAKEOUT

Look at your agreed-upon deliverables or expectations. Then look at your team or key stakeholders. Ask them, "How can I help you succeed in delivering on these elements we've agreed are important in our organization?"

CHALLENGE

Write down the name of one person you lead or one person who leads you. What is one thing you can do to help them succeed in their role this week? Go directly to them and ask, "How can I help you succeed?" Write it down, and then do it.

04
CHAPTER

> **HOW OFTEN DO OTHER PEOPLE'S RESPONSIBILITIES INFLUENCE YOUR LEADERSHIP?**

IT'S NOT MY RANCH

▶ When we lived in Montana, a friend of ours ran the maintenance team for a former-Air Force station there. He was fond of saying, "It's not my ranch."

People would bring him problems: issues from other teams or something they observed in passing, but if it wasn't his ranch, he wasn't changing his whole day to go fix it.

He saved his time, resources, and attention for what was. His ranch, his responsibility.

Your ranch is the scope of influence and responsibility you carry.

What is your ranch? What should you be concerned with?

Are you concerned with what someone else is doing when you need to deal with issues on your own ranch? How well do you know your ranch?

There are two dangers of not knowing our ranch.

First, We lower our level of influence. We abdicate responsibility. For example, imagine you accept someone else spent a significant portion of your budget for their purposes. Our ranch includes our budget and the influence those dollars carry.

Don't lower your influence by giving up your ranch.

Second, we exceed our level of influence. We embroil ourselves in matters we hold no responsibility for or cannot influence.

For example, comparing your role and opportunities within the organization to a peer's role and responsibilities from a different department. What they do with their time, how they spend their budget or the freedom they give to their staff is their ranch.

Don't outstrip your influence by moving off your ranch.

We have to learn to say, "It's not my ranch."

At the end of the day, we are responsible for our ranch. Know it inside and out, so when our ranch succeeds, we have the satisfaction of a job well done.

And if it's failing, we can see how to get our ranch back on its feet.

Do you know your ranch? Do you know the scope of your influence and responsibility?

IN
FLU
ENCE

TAKEOUT

Step up as a leader and own the influence and responsibility you carry. Know your ranch.

CHALLENGE

On a scale of 1-10, how well do you know your ranch?

On a scale of 1-10, how often (and on what) are you operating outside your influence and responsibility?

In what situations are you trying to operate on someone else's ranch? When do you need to say, "It's not my ranch"?

05
CHAPTER

> **WHAT HELPS YOU THINK FORWARD? TO SEE THE FUTURE POSSIBILITIES?**

IMPLICATIONAL THINKING

Look Ahead: What do you see?

▶ I have a friend who will put a pine cone on the desk while speaking or teaching.

He asks everyone, "What do you see?" Invariably he'll get "pine cone," "seeds," "a tree," or perhaps "a forest."

Then, he'll gaze across the room, building tension, and cry out, "CAN YOU HEAR THE MUSIC?"

He sees something no one else does. He sees potential in the distant future, from a pine cone to seeds, to trees in a forest, and ultimately, a wooden violin. He hears someone playing music.

Implicational thinking is thinking through the possible future consequences.

Try asking yourself:
- What happens if I do this?
- How might this decision affect operations in 18 months?
- What would this action do for our team if we embed it repeatedly during the next year?

Learn to see the consequences. Develop implicational thinking, see the seeds, imagine the forest, picture the violin. Hear the music.

The skill of implicational thinking is the most significant value-adding tool any leader can bring into an organization.

Implicational thinking applies to decision making. To systems. To policies.

At every level of every organization, we must cultivate the habit of implicational thinking.

To develop implicational thinking, look ahead.

Appraise any potential outcomes, repercussions, or reverberations. Make a better decision. Act accordingly.

Implicational thinking helps us to avoid negative outcomes and allows us to embrace a positive future.

So, what might be coming your way? Can you hear the music in your organization?

Do we understand how to THINK like someone who is expected to lead other people?

TAKEOUT

Leaders need to be future-focused and anticipate (where possible) the potential outcomes or impacts of decisions, actions, and behaviors.

CHALLENGE

Choose one 'bigger' decision you need to make this week. Write down 2-4 possible outcomes or impacts; the good, the bad, and the humorous. How does being aware of the options - the potential consequences - shift your implicational thinking?

06
CHAPTER

> **WHAT IS THE INFLUENCE OF YOUR INFLUENCE AS A LEADER?**

LEADERSHIP SHADOW

How broad is our Shadow? Who do we reach?

▶ Walking on the beach with my kids, we often play one of our favorite family games: Shadow Tag. The basic idea is to try and jump on everyone else's shadow and avoid getting your own shadow stood on. Lots of running and jumping and dodging ensues.

On the beach, a shadow is often well-defined; crisp, clear lines in the bright sunshine. There is a noticeable start and stop to the area of shadow. When we play the game, we are either in or out.

In life, we all have a leadership shadow.

A shadow of influence. A shadow of impact. A shadow of legacy.

Our leadership shadow is our influence's influence.

Our shadow is the ongoing - further than we ever anticipated - influence of our influence.

We all make decisions - positive or negative - which impact the lives of those around us. We cast a leadership shadow.

We often see a lot of impact from our leadership; staff impacted by our decision to give them a pay raise (we see their emotion often), the effect of clarity rising when we choose to make time to talk with our team, the impact of our decision to embrace an innovative idea.

The impact-type leadership shadow is most easily identified.

Harder to identify - and therefore harder to remain conscious of - are the dual leadership shadows of influence (in real-time) and legacy (long after we are gone).

One day I received the news of a friend's death. It was sudden and most definitely unexpected. And while I mourned his loss, to this day, I cherish, deeply, the legacy of his leadership.

I still walk in his shadow. I think, "What would He do here?" or "How would He respond now?"

Thankfully, His is a good leadership shadow.

Reflect: Who does your leadership shadow influence?

I also engage with people and situations casting a negative leadership shadow.

Excluding bullies and outright liars, a negative leadership shadow is usually more subtle, more demoralizing, and even more challenging to get rid of.

Indeed, we can influence our intended audience or perhaps attempt to clarify our impact. But ultimately, our leadership shadow will travel farther (and be much larger) than we ever thought possible.

With 125 million followers, Barak Obama is the most followed person on Twitter. I wonder what his leadership shadow looks like? The unintended, the legacy shadow?

Think about all the people you lead and work with. Picture their faces. Now think about their spouses and partners and kids and kids teachers. Think about their hairdresser or accountant or the checkout operator at the supermarket they just talked to.

Does your leadership - your communication and interaction and influence - does it cast a shadow on their lives too?

DO WE KNOW OUR INFLUENCE'S INFLUENCE?

DIG DEEPER AND LOOK WIDER

TAKEOUT

Our influences influence goes far beyond our line of sight. We have a choice and a responsibility to ensure - where possible - that we have a positive impact with our leadership shadow.

CHALLENGE

Write down the names of three people you know you influence. Now think about three more people they each influence. A simple circle of 12 people you're influencing. Consider what sort of influence you currently have and what is one thing you could do to ensure you have a positive impact?

07
CHAPTER

> **HOW DO WE MOTIVATE NEW BEHAVIORS, HABITS, AND ACTIONS FOR OURSELVES AND OTHERS?**

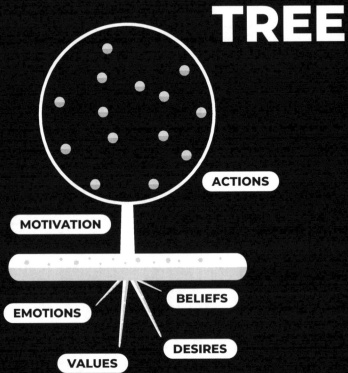

▶ I have a friend who is chronically late. He is late to work. He is late to events. He is late for everything.

"I'm sorry, but here's what happened..." is the introduction to every meeting.

Have you ever seen someone on your team do something and thought, "Why on earth are they doing that?" What on earth would motivate someone to make that decision?

Alternatively, have you ever tried to increase someone's motivation? Perhaps with an added incentive of pay or the promise of flex time for meeting the project deadline?

Think of Motivation like a fruit tree. As leaders or coworkers, all we see is action—the fruit. We get to see if someone has good fruit in their life. That crisp kind word or empathetic gesture, that show-up-early behavior we love to see. All we see is the end result.

Bad fruit is easy to see too. The rotten on the ground fruit of poor performance, minimal output, and snarky replies. Again, all we see is the end result.

As leaders, we often spend time analyzing the fruit (the action) we see around us. If it's good fruit, we want to replicate it. We try to scale it across an organization.

We use coaching, training, and development opportunities in an attempt to build new decision-branches for our employees with bad fruit. We try to shed light on the decision-making process and spell it out; 1-2-3.

Often, if we see bad fruit, we make an attempt to change the motivation-trunk. It's like we cut down the tree and graft a new trunk into place.

Slow performance? Offer a bonus incentive. Poor customer service? Offer a training incentive. High staff turnover? Offer a wage increase to those who stay.

In the short term, the motivation-trunk graft works. For a little while, people will respond to the offer of more money. Or they will reshape their actions while the attention is on them and their motivation.

But ultimately, the motivation graft fails because it does not deal with the roots. The roots produce the fruit.

It's true: Our consistent behavior comes from our unseen, hidden-below-the-surface root drivers.

Emotions. Values. Desires. Beliefs.

Take a team member who is habitually late, for example. No matter how much we attempt to change their motivation, long-term change will not occur if they genuinely believe being late is of little consequence.

Maybe they value "being present" to such a high degree that the idea of leaving the present to go to another future meeting 'on time' seems unconscionable.

Perhaps emotions drive their late action. A rough home life, pressure from extended family, or a chronically ill child, any of these could influence difficult behavior.

LOOK DEEPER

One day, my friend came to work, and his boss turned to him.

"Hey, how are you doing? Is everything alright at home?" said his boss.
"Yes, all good, thanks."
"How is your wife?"
"She's fine."
"Great, I'm glad to hear it. Are you sleeping ok?"
"I've had a few rough nights, but nothing that's a big problem."

"Ok great, well, to be honest, I need to talk to you about something. I've noticed that you are often late to work, and you have been skipping our team meeting. The younger guys on the team are watching you. They want to be like you; they really look up to you."

"When you're late or miss our meetings, you communicate to the entire team that their time isn't valuable, and their contribution isn't valuable."

"Did you mean to do that? You need to be here on time; I know you can do it."

My friend's boss took five minutes to have a clear conversation that was focused first on my friend and then on his work in a way that motivated and encouraged him. As a result, he learned to show up on time.

His boss took it to the next level and dug around a little bit, making sure there were not any pressing issues at home, and then went straight for a core question around values, desires, emotions, and beliefs: "Does what I do matter here?"

And then, he answered that question with a very clear "Yes."

Yes, it matters, yes what you do in this office matters to the team, and it matters to the whole organization.

WHAT YOU DO MATTERS

TAKEOUT

New actions, habits, and behaviors are always driven by something more profound. Leaders must learn to recognize and utilize emotions, desires, values, and beliefs when considering motivation.

CHALLENGE

Think of an existing or newly forming habit for yourself. What is one word in each category (emotions, values, desires, beliefs) motivating that habit?

08
CHAPTER

WHAT MAKES A PRACTICE "BEST" ANYWAY?

QUESTION BEST PRACTICE

▶ We've all been there. That moment in a meeting when someone interjects with a comment along the lines of "Well, best practice suggests we need to...."

The challenge of a best practice is that it's only best for the person or team who came up with the idea in the first place.

The best practice for a race car pit crew is different than for your local auto shop. And it's very different from your own garage!

The best practice of a Michelin-starred restaurant cannot compare to the best practice of a street-food stall. They have a different perspective—different criteria for success.

When we talk about Best Practice, we need to learn to ask, "from whose perspective using what criteria?"[†] Who said it is best practice? And when?

More importantly, is it the best practice for us right now with our available resources and in our given situation? Is this best for us? From whose perspective? And by what criteria?

[†] Michael Quinn Patton. *Evaluation, Knowledge Management, Best Practices, and High Quality Lessons Learned.* American Journal of Evaluation. 2001.

TAKEOUT

Benchmarking helps scale growth. In the right situations, it's helpful. But best practice may be different for individual organizations. What got them there might not get you there. So ask some questions. Explore. Find the criteria and perspective that works for you.

CHALLENGE

What elements of your leadership/operations are built on best practice? How are those practices still best for you? What might a new approach look like?

09
CHAPTER

> **WHAT AUTHORITY DO YOU HOLD? HOW DOES IT ALIGN WITH THE RESPONSIBILITIES OF YOUR ROLE?**

RESPONSIBILITY

AUTHORITY

▶ Responsibility: The duty to take action

Authority: The power to make decisions

There is a constant dance – an interplay between responsibility and authority in every leader's life.

Usually, we have a responsibility to ensure something takes place. The responsibility to see a project completed on time and on budget. The responsibility for the safety and well-being of our team. The responsibility for end-of-year outcomes.

No matter what our level in an organization, we carry a broad responsibility.

But authority – authority is naturally hierarchical. It goes up and down.

Too often, there is a disconnect between responsibility and authority. Usually, it is too much responsibility and not a consummate level of authority to match.

When you don't have the power to make decisions - to spend, start or stop, invest or divest; when you don't have authority - it's hard to do your job.

Imagine if you're the janitor.
If you don't have the authority to purchase a mop, something is wrong.

If you're out making sales calls, and you can't decide how much of a discount to give any client, any at all, something is wrong.

Authority and responsibility must go hand-in-hand.

TYRANNY	**ENGAGEMENT**
APATHY	**FRUSTRATION**

AUTHORITY (vertical axis)

RESPONSIBILITY (horizontal axis)

TAKEOUT

We all have some authority and some responsibility. To do our jobs well, we need to have the authority that matches our responsibilities. Make a list of your own with two columns: "Responsibilities" (The duty to take action) and "Authority" (The power to act and make decisions). Do you notice any gaps? What conversations might need to happen to close those gaps?

CHALLENGE

Focus on evaluating authority levels in your team.
How empowered are your people to produce decisions that make a meaningful difference?

10
CHAPTER

> **WHAT WAS THE LAST CRISIS YOU FACED AS A LEADER? WHERE DID IT COME FROM?**

DON'T BUILD A CRISIS

▶ A few years ago, we faced a constant crisis. Every. Single. Week.

A particular role had high turnover, highly transitional temp staff, and a massive day-to-day impact on our operations.

When I look back, our processes let us down. I knew this slightly; at the time, we dealt with some internal communication to help stem the turnover.

Yet, we failed to see the bigger picture of the crisis built on systemic processes.

We structured ourselves into a hole. We built ourselves a crisis.

How many of us walk through crises which could be avoided (or certainly lessened in impact) if we learned to adjust our processes?

Look at how often major airlines end up in the news when there is disagreement over handling situations.

Why? "Airline Policy." "Usual Practices." "It's a standard procedure when...." For airlines, their crises often emerge out of their processes.

When people talk about a leadership crisis, they're often saying, "Our processes have failed us, and it caught us out."

How often do our processes, our systems, lead us to the point of un-sustainability?

When you face a crisis, don't just deal with the symptoms.

Analyze the process you walked through to land you there. Then start at the beginning to rebuild, rather than just putting out fires.

Process analysis results in long-term solutions rather than knee-jerk reactions when things go wrong.

How can you evaluate your processes to not get caught in a crisis? How might different ways of working help you at this time of year?

Don't build yourself a crisis.

WHO
WHAT
WHEN
WHERE
WHY
& HOW

TAKEOUT

Be aware of what is influencing a crisis, especially an ongoing one. Consider what engrained processes have led to this point. Evaluate Who, What, When, Where, Why, and How to get some perspective, and hopefully some good answers. Analyze the process you need to walk through now so you don't build yourself a crisis.

CHALLENGE

What constantly feels under pressure in your sphere of influence? What processes contribute to that pressure? What is one minor adjustment you can take to step back from the edge of crisis?

WHAT IS MOST IMPORTANT TODAY?

— PART TWO —

CHAPTER 11

> **WHAT UNWRITTEN WAYS OF WORKING GAIN ATTENTION AND REINFORCEMENT IN YOUR WORLD?**

CELEBRITY

SERVICE

▶ Who is the biggest celebrity that you know? What are they like? How are they a celebrity? Why do people follow them?

Now think about the most outstanding servant you know. Who are they? What makes them so good at serving?

Last question: who would you rather have in your corner when life gets tough?

We have a culture moving like an out-of-control freight train toward the celebration of celebrity. High profile. Loud voices. Able to post prominent comments on every subject.

But the world is not changed by celebrities.

Servants change the world. Churchill. Eisenhower. Mother Teresa. Mandela.

We cannot afford to create celebrity leaders. I'd even argue celebrity leaders are not leaders at all. Leadership is about helping others succeed. So is service.

Leadership is about clarity of purpose, clarity of position, and clarity of priorities. So is service.

The world demands celebrity but desperately needs service.

If your organization is growing a celebrity leader: Stop.

To stop growing a culture of celebrity leadership, ask yourself:
Who did I call/message/talk to today, as a leader, to benefit their work (and not mine)?

To further clarify whether you (or the leaders around you) are moving toward celebrity or service, consider these contrasts:

1. The underlying question of success: "Who can help me succeed?" (celebrity) vs. "How can I help you succeed?" (service).

2. Communication and Celebration: Remains silent unless the 'win' is theirs (celebrity) vs. Celebrating the work of others (service).

3. Recognition and Reward: Only praises people for doing things right (celebrity) vs. Praising people for doing the right thing (service).

4. Future Growth and Change: Accepts any situation which makes them look good (celebrity) vs. Holds a healthy unhappiness with any situation which doesn't include all team members growing (service).

Bottom line: The world needs authentic leaders who know how to serve. The world needs you.

SERVE SOMEONE ELSE TODAY. CHANGE THEIR WORLD.

TAKEOUT

It is easy to accidentally reinforce a celebrity culture. But it is critical to support a service culture.

CHALLENGE

Pick one of the following areas: communication, recognition, future growth. Is service or celebrity currently leading the charge of influence in that area of your work?

12
CHAPTER

> **WHAT HOLDS YOUR TEAM GROUNDED IN THE PRESENT WHILE KEEPING YOUR EYES OPEN TO THE FUTURE?**

TWO CULTURES

▶ Aspirational Culture

I'm sure we've all seen plenty of cultural statements for organizations;
- on the wall behind reception
- buried in a policy manual
- printed on the classic team-fun-day T-shirt.

These statements are usually aspirational in nature. They point to how the CEO or Board or Executive Leadership Team wants the organization to behave.

Aspirational statements acknowledge: 'Hey, we're not always perfect, but we're moving in this direction.'

Most organizations are relatively close in their cultural statements to how most employees behave most of the time.

Hence, Aspirational: Close and always aspiring to work closer toward that goal.

Habitual Culture

Habitual culture is the unspoken, normalized behavior of employees—the day-to-day.

Often overlooked, these behaviors are acceptable by either the promotion of conduct or the absence of speaking against it.

We could say we value education, but do we invest in training for our staff? Would we make it easy for someone to go to graduate school part-time or take an art class?

We could say we value teamwork, but if the senior leadership team lives in an inaccessible bubble behind email, schedules, and the power-distance of responsibility, how valuable is teamwork?

What is your habitual culture like for the people you lead?

What cultural elements are easy or hard to recognize for you?

How will you invite input to see any blind spots in both aspirational and habitual culture?

"The culture of any organization is shaped by the worst behavior the leader is willing to tolerate."

Steve Gruenert and Todd Whitaker
School Culture Rewired. 2015.

TAKEOUT

The aspirational culture of an organization is easy to spot. It's usually written down and repeated often. Do not underestimate the influence of habitual culture. Keep an eye on the normal rules of ways of working. Ensure you positively reinforce what truly aligns with the culture you're trying to build.

CHALLENGE

Identify two elements of habitual culture in your organization. One positive. One negative. How might those elements influence the current output or future potential of your organization?

13
CHAPTER

> **WHAT DO YOU DO WITH FAULTS AND FAILURES?**

BLAME

[bleym] **verb: Be. Lame.**

▶ A friend of mine works for a large American insurance company. A few years ago, an employee caused an outage costing the company a million dollars an hour in downtime. Four hours (and $4 million) later, the issue was resolved.

Called before a board of VP's to explain the events— well, mostly the cost— my friend was asked whether he would now fire the employee? "Fire Him?" he asked surprised, "we just spent $4 million ensuring we never do this again."

It is easy to blame faults on employees.

Let me give you another scenario: Imagine John is late to work. You may think to yourself, "John is lazy," or "John is unable to manage his time," or "John cannot take responsibility."

The blame always falls on *who John is*.

Now, imagine you are late. You say to yourself, "My car battery was flat," or "The traffic was a nightmare," or "My kids are having trouble at school and only told me this morning."

The blame always falls on *your circumstances*.

Here's the truth: We blame our circumstances for our failures, while we blame the character of others for their failure.

We blame our failures on our circumstances while blaming others' failures on their character.

Employees are always to blame because they failed. We assume they are at fault. We often do not dig into circumstances surrounding any failure.

We will never help employees exceed our expectations if our default belief contains suspicion regarding their character. Learn to dig deeper and look a little wider.

The $4 million outage occurred because of a systems fault any employee could have triggered. The unlucky employee of the day did cost the company in finances and downtime.

He also saved the company the potential of millions more in damages by learning how to fix the problem and training others in the department too.

Stop blaming your employees' character. Start working with them in search of solutions.

You hired good people. Trust them.

If mistakes happen, join with them in exploring circumstances, managing environments, and pursuing future excellence — together.

How might blame be keeping you from leading effectively?

START WORKING WITH PEOPLE IN SEARCH OF SOLUTIONS

YOU HIRED GOOD PEOPLE. TRUST THEM.

TAKEOUT

We all encounter life circumstances beyond our control. What matters is how we respond as leaders.

CHALLENGE

Pay attention to your thinking this week. Listen to your own words or internal monologue.

Who or what is receiving unnecessary negative attention?

CHAPTER 14

HOW PREPARED ARE YOU FOR PRESSURE SITUATIONS?

PRETENDING IS

PRACTICING

▶ In 2019, when New Zealand Police reacted swiftly to a terror attack in Christchurch, many of those officers came directly from a training session where they discussed active-shooter scenarios.

The training session was not a field exercise. Officers did not run around a building using stun grenades and blank rounds. The training was a gathering of police officials discussing tactics and learning from one another.

In essence, it was pretending. Pretend is a gross over-simplification. Yet I imagine their conversations went something along the lines of, "Pretend this happens, what should we do?" Or "In this pretend scenario, let's discuss actions and implications."

Within moments of receiving the emergency call, officers applied their "pretending" to a real-life situation.

A day of pretending was actually a day of practice.

When we gather a group of leaders to discuss conflict resolution or role-play a customer service situation, our pretending is practicing.

When we use virtual reality to help customers pretend they're using our products - their pretending is practicing.

There is untold learning value in role-playing. There is untold educational gain from picturing yourself applying training material.

Never underestimate the value of learning and "pretend."

Discipline from the OUTSIDE is doomed to fail if not met with a desire from the INSIDE.

MEASURE
UNDERSTAND
IMPROVE
REPEAT

TAKEOUT

Role-play. Envision. Imagine what might happen. Anticipate actions and reactions. Pretend. Above all, prepare yourself and your team for the opportunities or challenges ahead. Use practice and pretend scenarios to prepare your team for pressure situations. Give them practice in areas where they will face pressure in the future.

CHALLENGE

What is one skill you're currently focused on developing? How might some pretending - some situational practice - set you up for success moving forward?

15
CHAPTER

> **HOW DO YOU PROVOKE ACTION?**

URGE

[ˈəːdʒ] verb: Go. Move.

▶ When I started training and speaking internationally, a mentor urged me to pause for an intensive 9-month study period.

I thought it would hurt my fledgling influence; He said it would exponentially increase my impact. His urge was right.

I had the opportunity to step into a senior leadership role at an age much younger than comparative leaders. Again, my leaders urged me to consider the impact I could make as a young leader.

The urge proved true.

The word 'urge' carries the potential to unlock lives and stories, and opportunities. Urge those around you to step up.

Daily life does not require the use of this powerful word. Not every opportunity mandates a leadership urge forward.

But when the right time comes along, when used wisely, "Urge" has the power to unlock incredible leadership potential.

TAKEOUT

The right word, in the right situation, is incredibly powerful for unlocking potential. Try using the word "urge" with a key staff member (or even on yourself). When you are urged to move, respond well and see what opportunities open up.

CHALLENGE

Look at the people in your sphere of influence. Who could benefit from being urged, and how? Have a quick conversation and urge them to move forward this week.

16
CHAPTER

WHAT DOES A HEALTHY LEADERSHIP LIFE LOOK LIKE?

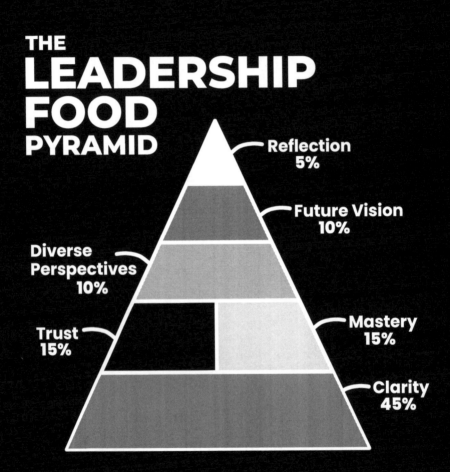

▶ My first introduction to the healthy food pyramid idea was around age ten.

It was one of those pre-teen classes where you're smart enough to think but not sharp enough to raise any serious objections to what's taught.

Our teacher explained that we should eat more fruit and veg and lay off the high-sugar snacks.

All I remember taking from that class was it is okay to eat high-sugar snacks every day.

Healthy leadership requires a healthy balance of intake: We need a Leadership Food Pyramid.

The Leadership Food Pyramid focuses primarily on our intake as leaders, what we're drawing in, how we use our time, and where our focus needs to lean.

However, similar percentages and areas of focus must become our outbound effort also. It is a balanced intake and output.

WHAT IS YOUR LEADERSHIP INTAKE?

Clarity

The most significant leadership food intake we need as leaders centers around clarity.

Leaders must spend a significant proportion of time focusing on gaining clarity of purpose, position, and priorities.

Only when we are clear why we're doing what we're doing, clear on where we are in relation to our goals/competitors/budget/etc., and clear on what needs doing in what order can we begin to free ourselves up to lead.

THE GREAT LEADERSHIP CHALLENGE: GAINING CLARITY

The greatest challenge of leadership is getting clarity first before succumbing to the tyranny of the urgent or the distractions of the frivolous.

Make time for clarity.

Mastery

As leaders, we don't have to be the best in the room at everything.

Seriously, hire people who are so good at what they do, it scares you a little bit.

While we don't have to be the best, we must carry a degree of competence and skill. Perhaps more importantly, it is crucial as leaders, we hold a willingness to improve our skills. As we grow in leadership, the competence needed for our role(s) may change, so we must change too.

Our field of expertise may experience a radical shift due to technology or external demands. So keep up with the times.

What is the 1% better we can improve?

In leading others, consider what up-skilling is needed to keep your team ahead of any coming changes or to make a value-adding investment in their career/life/growth. Value your people by contributing to their mastery. It builds trust too.

Trust

As leaders, we cannot underestimate the importance of giving and receiving trust. It is the foundation of any high-performing team, and its absence is the root cause of any team dysfunction.

Trust is a two-way street. Leaders rise and fall on the trust they create and carry.

We give trust to those we lead. We trust our staff to complete assigned roles; to follow through on commitments. We trust them to engage in their leadership journey of clarity, mastery, etc.

We receive trust also. It is often called ownership.

We receive explicit trust through leadership positions or our meeting of the expectations of those around us. We own our role and our outcomes to build trust continuously.

We receive implicit trust through our actions, the clarity we provide, and the competence we bring to situations. It is a shared acceptance of an authority to make decisions.

Diverse Perspectives

What is the last book you read that stretched your thinking? What podcasts expand your understanding of our diverse world?

Who do you look forward to a coffee conversation with because you know it will leave you thinking differently about yourself, your situation, or your impact on humanity?

Healthy leadership requires a healthy intake of diverse perspectives.

Read, Talk, Listen, Study, Watch. Do whatever it takes to intentionally invite diverse perspectives to shape, adjust, challenge, expand, and form your thinking.

Since the time of the Roman Empire, great leaders have been great readers. The pursuit of diverse knowledge has inevitably led to leadership positions. We have no excuses for not engaging in the crucial work of growing our leadership perspective.

"The task of the educated mind is simply put: read to lead."

- Cicero 106-43 B.C.

Future Vision

I once heard it said that managers focus on doing things right, while leaders focus on doing the right things.

It is the pursuit of "doing the right things" which propels leaders to a future-focused positioning.

Always in pursuit of a little bit better. Always in pursuit of an innovative solution. Always looking for an opportunity to engage in an emerging market.

A healthy leadership food pyramid means we must spend time looking to the future, whether to capture an opportunity positively or to ward off the impending impact of a challenging situation.

Healthy leaders look and lean forward into the future.

WHAT DOES THE FUTURE HOLD?

Reflection

Reflection is an essential component of a healthy Leadership Food Pyramid.

Intentional reflection, for as little as 15 minutes a day, has the potential to lift our improvement by 21%.[†]

Who wouldn't want to improve by 21%?

Too often, we exclude reflection; it requires too much of our time or is only for executive leaders with a personal assistant to clear their schedule.

For the ultra-stubborn Type-A leaders, reflection can often be seen as a weak-feeling-based activity. Best to get cracking with the day, right? Wrong.

Reflection is essential for healthy leadership. Reflection on clarity (Purpose, Position, Priorities). Reflection on trust. Reflection on mastery. Reflection on diverse perspectives. Reflection on the future.

Great leaders – healthy leaders – make time to reflect.

[†] Giada Di Stefano and Francesca Gino and Gary Pisano and Bradley R. Staats. *Making Experience Count: The Role of Reflection in Individual Learning.* Harvard Business School NOM Unit Working Paper No. 14-093. 2016.

SO YOU THRIVE

TAKEOUT

Healthy leaders require a healthy intake of the essentials: clarity, mastery, trust, diverse perspectives, future vision, and reflection. As leaders, if our focus isn't on these areas, what is it on? How can we get back to focusing on the things that really matter for our flourishing?

CHALLENGE

Look at your calendar for the coming week. Using the Leadership Food Pyramid as a rough guide, focus the activities in your week. How do your plans line up? Do you need to add in some diverse perspectives or reflection time? Is there anything excess you need to remove? Develop a healthy leadership intake for the coming week.

17
CHAPTER

WHAT IS TOXIC FOR YOUR TEAM?

*The following chapter is satire. It is designed to be comical and thought-provoking. Do not apply literally.

HOW TO BE A

TOXIC BOSS

▶ Step One: Ignore the work of your people.

Ignorance is essential. The more you can make your team feel insignificant, disregarded, and generally worthless, the more toxic you will be.

When someone finishes a project, pretend you didn't see it. If it's a task you delegated, your silence will only add to their shame and general lack of self-worth. Don't comment on any tasks, whether the finish quality, effort involved, or overall outcomes.

To increase the power of Step One, pretend their ideas are your ideas and attribute their project wins to yourself.

Do anything to diminish the true impact of their hard work.

If you work in an office building, be sure to keep the door to your personal space shut. Failing that, position your workspace in such a way that it sends a big "Get Lost!" toward anyone bold enough to approach.

If you lead a remote team, don't call them. Ever.

Be absent even when you're present online. Zoom is not the time for eye contact and connection. Maybe mix up their names or forget what their role is.

Reschedule often. Cancel 1:1 meetings. Don't show up.

Crucially, the goal is to flatten any ounce of extra effort or spark of joy within your team. Be Toxic.

THE TRUE IMPACT OF THEIR HARD WORK

Step 2:
Find failure, fault, and flaws.

No one is perfect, and it's your job to point out how.

A great Toxic Boss can pinpoint the most insignificant lapse in perfection and then dial it up to DEFCON-4.

Seriously, divert attention from your own work by loudly drowning out your team for being human. To be the most toxic, offer no coaching.

Guidance is strictly prohibited.

Training, up-skilling, and career development plans have no place in the world of a Toxic Boss.

Ideally, your team should have only a vague sense of what's required of them. Clear expectations are for the weak. If they can't figure it out, you are not a parent, babysitter, or game-show lifeline for them to call.

If you're hiring, wildly over-promise. Make it sound like coming to work will be Disneyland meets the United Nations. Full of Fun-loving World-changers.

That way, any failure to actually change the world is obviously their fault.

Blame and abdication are the salt and pepper of a Toxic Boss. The toxic spice of life.

Shift all responsibilities outward to others, but be sure to keep the authority for decision-making firmly in your seat. Make it very difficult - if not impossible - to get anything done.

Ask "Why?" a lot (but not in a helpful way!). Use a tone that suggests a mix of disinterest, disdain, and despair.

This is an excellent opportunity to point out any and all flaws. There will be many.

Under no circumstances should you celebrate success. None. A true Toxic Boss only celebrates themselves.

WHAT DID YOU DO WITH THE FLAWS YOU FOUND TODAY?

Step 3: Be Right. Always.

If possible, talk over the top of people. And definitely, absolutely, shoot down their ideas.

At every opportunity, speak up and step in to tell them how you could do it better. Point out how to do the job right. Use lots of detail with specific examples from your own success.

Drop a running commentary on how their peers are doing with their work. Be completely unfair in your approach.

Talk smack, belittle, and complain. But only to their face: in public, keep them off guard by using subtle praise (but don't ignore Step One in the process!).

Keep everyone suspicious, create unnecessary silos, and withhold information - all information. Power struggles are the super-food of the Toxic Boss.

To be genuinely toxic, fail to account for any situational context that might affect those you're leading. Covid is not an excuse. People's lives do not matter. Avoid personal connection wherever possible.

Ignorance is bliss. The weekend activities, significant career milestones, or the life-altering births/deaths/marriages of your team do not concern you.

Humor is the Toxic Boss' best friend. Even if no one is laughing, you should bring in a joke or two to keep people from feeling they can ignore you. The best Toxic Bosses use humor to communicate crucial operational information, adding to the day-to-day confusion (See Step Two for details).

Even if you change your mind, you were right all along. Never apologize for your greatness.

TAKEOUT

Self-awareness goes a long way as a leader. Very few people actually *want* to be a toxic boss, so step up your own awareness. Ask yourself, "What might I be doing - unintentionally - that is toxic for my team?"

CHALLENGE

Go back through the chapter and consider the opposite actions to the toxic behavior described. Imagine what a good leader would do. Then, go do that. Don't actually become a toxic boss.

18
CHAPTER

> **HOW CAN YOU HELP YOUR TEAM DEAL WITH CHANGE?**

WHAT DOES THIS CHANGE MEAN FOR ME?

▶ Do you remember your first promotion? Maybe it was via a phone call, in an office meeting room, or virtually online. Do you remember that moment?

The nervous excitement you suddenly feel. You finally receive the acknowledgment of your hard work. A subtle smile plays across your face as you accept the new role. That "Oh wow!!" moment you experience as the weight of responsibility sinks in.

Then comes the part where we tell our friends and coworkers that we got a promotion. That we're now "The Boss."

Most often, a promotion comes because we're good at what we do. We produce x-number of widgets or outcomes faster, better, and more efficiently than our peers.

The What of what we do stands out. So we're promoted.

Upon promotion, a subtle shift begins to take place. What we do is no longer the central measure of our success. We move from personal output to achieving success through the outcomes of others.

How they do What they do becomes our key priority.

During all this change - the excitement of the new role, the uncertain weight of responsibility, all of it - there is a core question we must continue to ask.

More importantly, it's a question our peers are asking as we begin to transition into leading them.

"What does this change mean for me?"

When our team asks: "What does this change mean for me?" within their role, it could mean:

- Supporting a new manager in being successful.
- Navigating the uncertainty of role shifts and the to-be-expected operational muddle-ups.
- Pressing into clarifying communication, not assuming the newly promoted manager knows everything (even if they were recently a peer).

Make a point of telling your team, "Hey, here's a question (whether we know it or not) we're all asking: 'What does this change mean for me?'"

Then talk through the answers of the question. Explore the outcomes and how they're affecting your team.

When we ask, "What does this change mean for me?" for ourselves, it could mean:

- Our team might develop new inside jokes without us.
- We might need to find new colleagues to problem-solve challenging work situations (someone on the same organizational level as us).
- Starting to fully own the responsibilities of the new role and gaining clarity on outcomes.
- Working hard to support our old peers to be successful.

Consistently ask, "What does this change mean for me?" for six months as you begin leading peers.

Ask it regarding the big picture. Also, ask it when you need to clarify the details of operations or people dynamics.

Recognize that the first answer to this question may not be the final answer - keep asking. Over time, you will gain clarity, communicate well, and lead your peers effectively.

GROWTH IS SPELLED C-H-A-N-G-E

TAKEOUT

During times of change, everyone asks the same question, "What does this change mean for me?" How does it affect my work or life, or routines? Take time to consider what any change means for your team and discuss it with them.

CHALLENGE

Look at one specific change happening in your world. Choose one person to have a conversation with this week - it could be a peer, a manager above you, or someone you lead. With them in mind, ask the question, "What does this change mean for me?" and explore the answers together.

CHAPTER 19

WHAT HAPPENS IF PEOPLE ARE PROMOTED TOO EARLY?

THE GOLDEN GOOSE OF MANAGEMENT

▶ In the classic tale of the Golden Goose, a young man named Simpleton finds a golden goose. Everyone else who tries to touch it ends up stuck to the goose and to each other. Everyone wants a piece of the action only to find they're stuck fast together.

Management is our modern golden goose. Lauded as desirable, we push employees to rise through the ranks. Being good at a job means leading others to do that job.

Too often, people are not trained how to manage others as they rise in ranking. Therefore they are stuck.

A friend of mine recently escaped the golden goose. As a police officer with 15+ years of experience, he rose to a management position over 30 guys. He successfully recognized his skills did not lean toward management; his skills were in the job. Taking a specialist role with another unit, he succeeded in creating space to excel in his skills.

What would change in our organizations be if we pushed people to excel in their skills rather than management? For upward mobility of skills and experience that doesn't include management?

TAKEOUT

Leadership or management is not for everyone. How do we genuinely help people grow and develop - excelling in their skills - without creating a golden goose scenario? Consider alternate forms of upward mobility for your team beyond the management of others.

CHALLENGE

Moment of truth: How equipped are you for the role you're currently in? On a 1-10 scale, how confident and how capable are you to lead? What skills need developing yourself, so you don't get stuck?

CHAPTER 20

HOW ARE PERSONAL VALUES INFLUENCED BY SEASONS OF LIFE?

PERSONAL VALUES LIFE CYCLE

60+ Legacy
Evergreen Projects
Investing in the Future
Long-term Impact

0-5 Nurture
Bonding
Security
Early Development

5-20 Educate
Formal Training
Team Sports
Community Clubs

20-30 Explore
Early Career
Travel
Network Building

30-60 Outwork
Full Career
Family and Children
Community Impact

▶ Since the first dedicated issue in 1947, TIME Magazine has produced over 45 covers focused on Generations.

Where will the babies of today be in the future? How will graduates cope in the world? Why are twenty-somethings focused on themselves? What happens in life after 50?

The corresponding articles seek to predict and explain behavior based on generational values. They suggest that because ABC generation values EFG specifically, then XYZ conduct must also occur, now or sometime in the future.

Exploring the outworking of values is not a recent phenomenon.

Aristotle (384-322 BC) described young people in his time, saying, "They think they know everything, and are always quite sure about it."† Aristotle's quote is not out of place in our modern world. Yet, it reveals an age-old sore spot concerning inter-generational understanding.

From Aristotle's time until the 21st Century, personal values have remained relatively similar in every generation.

---

† *The Works of Aristotle Translated into English Vol. XI: Rhetorica.* W. Rhys Roberts (Trans). 1924.

Safety. Security. Love. Adventure. Risk. Creativity.

Where differences between generations arise, it's more to do with age-and-stage of life, with how people live their lives, rather than the values themselves.

Think of personal values as a lifecycle. At 0-5 years old, we value nurture. We learn about safety and security and love and food and sleep and how to walk.

As we transition to formal education, we're taught values by our education system, family members, or sports clubs until we end school at roughly age 20.

Through our 20's we're on a journey to explore the world – we're trying to figure out our values. Not the ones we grew up with, but the ones we want to OWN ourselves. We build networks, begin a career, or begin multiple times over on multiple careers.

Then, for most of our working life, we focus on outworking our values in all of life. We try to hold steady to our values in the long career of our work. We raise families. We seek to impact our community.

Lastly, post-retirement, we focus more on leaving a legacy: on passing values to others by investing in the next generations.

Think of it this way: If we happen to be at a life stage where we're trying to outwork our values (30-60) or maybe looking to leave a legacy (60+), while the people we've newly hired as graduates (20-30) are trying to explore their values, then there is potential for miscommunication and misalignment.

That misalignment could be around what values we consider valuable, or they could be on how to outwork a particular value.

Maybe you're asking questions about your team, such as: Why would they ever leave this great organization? Why aren't they more committed?

Or perhaps, Why won't they just do things as we've always done? Why do I feel like I am parenting my team?

Try stepping back: What stage of life are you in?

What stage of life is your teammate in? And what can you do to build understanding and create clear communication?

TAKEOUT

We all have values. And all values matter. Sometimes the season of our lives influences the degree to which we focus on a particular set of values or how those values become outworked.

CHALLENGE

Look at the season of life you're currently in. What do you notice about how you emphasize certain values? Look at the season of life you're in with your role or career too. Consider those you are leading and following; how do their values align with yours? How do they differ? Is there a possibility that value differences you are experiencing relate to the stage of life you are each in?

WHAT IS ONE **MEANINGFUL ACTION** YOU CAN TAKE TODAY?

— PART THREE —

CHAPTER 21

HOW DO YOU KNOW IF SOMEONE CAN HANDLE RESPONSIBILITY?

THE
1 ft
FENCE

OF RESPONSIBILITY

▶ When the rock band Van Halen toured the USA in the 1980s, their production was the largest rock and roll show on tour. Over 850 lights, tons of equipment, and staging. It was a massive production.

Buried in the contractual requirements – the rider – within all the things to do with food and drinks supposed to be backstage in the dressing room was this line:

M & M's. (WARNING: ABSOLUTELY NO BROWN ONES).

This is a 1ft fence.

Van Halen didn't hate brown M&M's. Rather, it was a quick and simple check to see if the host venue had read all the details within the contract or not.

Brown M&M's were not an issue of life and death, but the weight of the equipment could have been if the stage failed.

In one Colorado show, the host promoters didn't read the contract (brown M&M's on the table), and the Van Halen road crew knew they needed to double-check everything. The heavy stage sank through the flooring and caused over $80K in damage.

A 1ft fence is a trigger that helps us gauge where people are at when we delegate.

The 1ft fence helps us know if people can handle responsibility. It also helps us see if we can avoid more significant issues later down the line.

As we increase our leadership influence journey, we'll find we don't always trust everyone at the same level. We see people in the same roles at different levels.

It could be because of training. Or perhaps because of how long they have spent with our company. It could be because of how complicated the task we're delegating to them is.

A 1ft fence is easy to get over. At the same time, if you're not watching where you're going, it's easy to fall over it too!

A 1ft fence is a trigger. It is a mini-test.

As leaders, it's not for us to use and say, "Haha, I caught you out!" but rather to help us know where people are at (and how we can help them succeed).

A 1ft fence could be watching to see who comes already ready to get working on Monday morning.

They know the plan for the day.

It could be a simple project, important but with minimal consequences.

To create a 1ft fence, choose something that will not ruin the business if it's not done but will also reveal something about those who take responsibility.

How could a 1ft fence help you this week?

M & M's

WARNING: ABSOLUTELY NO BROWN ONES.

TAKEOUT

Use mini-test moments - the 1ft fence - to consider whether people are ready for increasing responsibility. Like an early-warning system, gauge the important (to you) indicators of someone being prepared for the next leadership level.

CHALLENGE

What is one area of responsibility you could begin to pass to someone else? And what is the 1ft fence you need to set in place so you're aware when someone on your team might be ready to step up?

22
CHAPTER

> **HOW CAN YOU DELEGATE WITH CLARITY?**

INTENT VS. IMPACT

▶ Imagine $2 billion a year in revenue.

It is a lot to manage. A friend of mine did it for a while, running a company with hundreds of stores across the nation. His view on delegation changed my life:

Intent vs. Impact.

Often, we delegate a task to someone (clean the storeroom, finish the financial report, or prepare that presentation for the board) without being clear on the impact we're looking to see.

We give an outcome, but it's not specifically clear on the impact we expect.

Then, if the task seems to be going off script, we step into the process—micromanaging our staff—attempting to steer their work toward our "ideal" goal.

Our dilemma comes when we communicate an intent (what we want them to do) but not the impact (end-goal outcome) that we want to see.

As leaders, we must engage in the hard work of clearly identifying the impact our projects need to have.

Don't delegate an intention for the storeroom to be clean.

Instead, delegate the impact of a storeroom where every item is clearly labeled and easily accessible; a room where a five-year-old could find anything.

Don't delegate the intent of a complete financial report.

Delegate the impact of report any employee can understand. And does.

Don't delegate a presentation at a conference.

Delegate the life change you want attendees to apply as they walk away.

Think about the last project or responsibility you delegated: Was it an intent? Or an impact?

How can you go back and clarify some meaningful impact now?

Think about an upcoming project or deadline: What sort of impact are you looking to see? And who on your team also needs to know that impact?

WHAT IS THE OUTCOME WE'RE REALLY LOOKING FOR?

TAKEOUT

When you delegate, talk clearly about the impact you expect to see. What is the outcome you're after? What is the end result, and how will someone know they've been successful in reaching it?

CHALLENGE

Look at a task you're planning to give to someone else this week. Are you communicating intent or impact? How might a reframe create greater clarity and a better outcome?

CHAPTER 23

HOW DO YOU GIVE FEEDBACK WHEN PRESSED FOR TIME?

MICRO
FEEDBACK

▶ It is safe to say that almost everybody in every organization has played with LEGO bricks of some variety.

A young child can hold up their creation at every step of the building process and check if it looks like the instructional picture. It is visual microfeedback.

Microfeedback allows staff to learn in real-time. In a short space of time, we can acknowledge current work and offer steps for future growth.

Microfeedback allows us to appreciate performance and seek areas of improvement.

Think of microfeedback as a post-it note — concise and current action information.

In 30 seconds or less, we can give helpful advice for maturity and improvement. Literally between the car door and the office door.

Embrace little opportunities for transformational growth.

TAKEOUT

Regular microfeedback - quick, real-time input - helps everyone know where they're performing well and identify improvement opportunities. Keep microfeedback small (specific), recent, and with a clear picture of what "good" looks like.

CHALLENGE

Think of two people you work with regularly. What have you seen them do recently where a 30-second microfeedback conversation might lift and shift their performance? Have that conversation this week to help them succeed.

24
CHAPTER

> **WHAT TYPE OF COMMUNICATION DOES MY TEAM NEED RIGHT NOW?**

SMOKE, FLAGS, & ROCKETS

HOW URGENT IS OUR COMMUNICATION?

▶ One of the most famous paintings in American history depicts George Washington crossing the Delaware River on his way to liberate the colonies from the King of England.

George is standing on the bow with a commanding presence. The entire painting exudes "This is a Historical Moment." Surrounding Washington - in both the fore and background - is a litany of Smoke and Flags, and you can almost imagine the Rockets in the background.

So, what sort of signals do we send to our people?

Smoke

Smoke is the communication that is always there in an organization.

It's the water-cooler talk; it's the unofficial staff message system (and there always is one!); it's the general chatter around operations.

Smoke has variety. It could be thick smoke, thin smoke, any color of the rainbow smoke.

We need to recognize that smoke is pervasive. We cannot control smoke once it's out there for the world to see.

We have limited influence on the water-cooler talk. The back channels via Slack and Messenger are beyond us. So is the meeting after the meeting in the hallway. To influence smoke-communication, be aware of what you put into it.

Smoke has an incredible impact. At its best, smoke-communication is an excellent channel of information dissemination, a trustworthy source. At its worst, smoke-communication fosters unhealthy dialogue, breeds discontent, and undermines trust.

What sort of smoke does your organization have?

Flags

Flags are intentional. They're specific. Each one is structured and recognizable.

Skulls and crossbones? Pirate flag. Stars and Stripes? American flag. Big red leaf? Canada.

We know and recognize flags.

In the same way, we have formalized, recognizable, structured communication channels within organizations.

Flags are the weekly all-hands meeting or the daily 15-min stand-up.

Flags are also emails or formal app-based communication networks (Slack, Teams, etc.).

Flags are the ways in which the board decides to disseminate information down and out through an organization.

Think clear and specific. Timely. Regular channels.

Question to ponder: Can people accurately see the flags in your organization?

Also, are your flags old and faded?

Seriously, why are people still using email and reply-all for team communication?

Do you need to invest in new flags (systems and structures)?

CAN PEOPLE CLEARLY SEE YOUR FLAGS?

Rockets

Rockets scream action. They're loud and flashy and exciting—rockets impact.

Rockets are your emergency meeting or text message system.

Rockets are the shouted-voice through the office—cutting through the chatter and drawing attention.

Rockets are flashing lights and full work-stop action.

There is a place in every business for rocket communication.

A fire. Literally, fire in the building or an accident costing lives or millions of dollars. A decision that might end up sinking the ship.

Fire off that rocket!!!

However, not everything is loud and over-bright and urgently needs to move through the organization.

Monthly performance down? Not a rocket. Is manufacturing held up for a day by supply issues? Not usually a rocket, either.

These are flags. What's needed here is clarity—not shouting.

Use rockets sparingly.

Are you trying to find out what your staff thinks of the parking space allocations? Smoke. Definitely smoke.

Be cautious when starting emails with "Urgent," "Priority," and "Must Read." Evaluate the rockets you're trying to send.

But if you're 50% over budget (or even 10% - you be the judge) and you're 25% off the pace on delivery - go ahead - rocket. Genuine Emergency? Again, rocket away!

Smoke, flags, and rockets are just metaphors. Communication within an organization involves so much more.

But maybe learn to ask, "what do my rockets communicate to my team?"

What is your default style? What about your team or your organization? Is it Smoke, Flags, or Rockets?

And ultimately, how could you reset your communication to reflect what actually needs to get out to your people?

TAKEOUT

Smoke, Flags, and Rockets is a metaphor for systems of communication present in every organization. What do our systems, how regularly we use them, and the degree of intensity involved communicate to our teams? Are our systems fit for purpose or not?

CHALLENGE

Think about the last month and take 15 minutes to look at your smoke, flags, and rockets. What do you notice? What is getting the most use? What might need some further evaluation? And what do you really want to be communicating?

CHAPTER 25

HOW DOES REFRAMING FLEXIBILITY BETTER SERVE YOUR TEAM?

▶ Flexibility in the workplace is often limited to the utopia of an extra day off.

Which usually means Friday. Or at least half of Friday.

Flexibility is the question of "How much will it bend before it breaks?"

Think about it: Aircraft wings are flexible. Testing during design includes load stress, maneuvering, flight angles, and turbulence, all to prove the wing's flexibility. It's an exercise in "will it break?"

In the same way, typical workplace flexibility revolves around bending but not broken. "How much can we bend our work hours before we break?"

Whether it's broken productivity or broken team cohesion, we often use a break-point to define flexibility. It's like asking, "what can I do outside of normal expectations before I find myself in trouble?"

What if we reframe Flexibility to Possibility? Instead of asking, "what might break?" we start asking, "What might be possible?"

What might be possible with a few more options? Maybe around benefits or a few more options around scheduling?

What new ways of engagement might we come up with? What unique value can we create from exploring a shift from flexible to possible?

Look at coffee shops. Cafes don't just offer Black Coffee and White Coffee. They offer options. They offer possibilities.

Coffee shops offer the possibility of connecting your drink with how you feel. The possibility of a better day (once you wake up!). The possibility of choosing for yourself.

Sometimes, we can't explore a possibility: it is not good to experiment with options while doing open-heart surgery.

Yet if we look a little at the world around us, I bet we'll find space for some possibility within our workplaces. For example, a vacation instead of a pay raise, lowering student debt for our team, or advanced resources for specific roles.

If you're moving roles, stop asking what companies offer in terms of flexibility and start asking about possibility. Help companies dream about what's possible.

Next time the word flexibility comes up in conversation, mentally reframe it to possibility and see what happens.

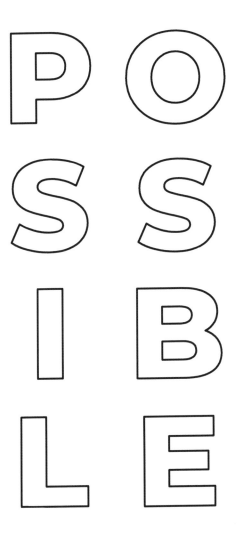

TAKEOUT

Start considering the possibilities. What new opportunities to innovate, explore, and re-invent are around the corner? Go further - Look at what might be possible.

CHALLENGE

Take any one element you regularly hear people wanting flexibility - pay, hours, bonuses, work location, etc. - and ask yourself, "What possibilities might a shift in this area bring for our team?"

26
CHAPTER

WHAT KILLS MOMENTUM IN YOUR MEETINGS?

HIDDEN MEANINGS

THE STATEMENT BEHIND THE STATEMENT

▶ I sat in the bright boardroom, leaning back in an office chair. Our meeting had droned on - already running overtime - and we were stuck.

Ideas had been flowing well until "it" came. The conversation dead-end, ushered in by one of our senior leaders.

"We've tried that before."

Silence filled the room, and I could feel the ideas and momentum slipping out the door as we sat there suddenly stagnated.

Well, they'd tried it. They - the more experienced, smarter, wiser ones - had tried it, and it hadn't worked, so that was it—a dead end.

"We've tried that before."
"We can't do that!"
"Don't they know that's not going to work?!?!"
"This sucks"

These four statements - and hundreds of others just like them - are absolute statements at face value.

Definitive outbursts against the possibility of progress.

They are statements that create dead-ends in conversations or, worse, cul-de-sacs in progress.

Yet, these four statements have another unexplored similarity. The Hidden Meaning: The statement behind the statement.

What sucks? The timing of something? The way it's communicated? The expectations within the situation? The level of difficulty? The outcome projected?

We cannot do what? Which part of the issue at hand appears undoable?

Whose permission is required (or assumed to be required) to take action? Is it the ended end-result that appears impossible?

We've tried what before? All of it or only part of the current proposal? And under what circumstances? Who was involved, and what skills did they bring into play during that earlier attempt?

What is the statement behind the statement?

Underneath a surface statement there is another world to explore.

As leaders, we must do the work of questioning the statement behind the statement. Take time to notice when an absolute statement comes up.

Pause. Reflect. Is there something else going on behind the scenes or below the surface?

Positive statements have a "Statement behind the Statement," too. I had some feedback on a presentation once which said, "That was great!"

What does "That was great!" actually mean? Was the timing perfect? Was the content magnificent?

If we're willing to ask a little deeper, unpacking the first statement, we often find some golden truth to help us grow and improve.

What statements are often thrown around in your sphere of influence?

Maybe it's something in your sports club or team? Perhaps it is something in your workplace? Or could it be something your kids say around the dinner table every night?

What does a statement actually mean? What is the statement behind the statement?

The next time an absolute statement kills the discussion at your meeting, don't let it slip by. Ask a question, make a pivot, push in instead of leaning back.

Try asking a question that begins with two little words, "which part."

"Which part" have you tried before? "Which part" can we not do?

Try asking, "What elements of such-and-such seem difficult to do over?"

And my favorite question of all: "What makes that statement important right now? Unpack that for me."

As you do, you'll begin to build a culture where clarity is king and there are no hidden meanings.

BUILD A CULTURE WHERE CLARITY IS KING

TAKEOUT

If we're not careful, a 'throw away' statement in a conversation will end discussion and innovation. When you know this has happened, sit back and evaluate: What is the statement behind the statement? How might analyzing the hidden meaning create space for a shift in the conversation or forward momentum?

CHALLENGE

Pay attention to the next meeting you attend. What sort of "dead-end" statements do you hear? Write them down. What do you notice? Consider if there is something to explore - to create a new direction - behind those statements.

27
CHAPTER

HOW DO YOU ASK QUESTIONS THAT CHANGE THE WORLD?

WHAT MIGHT BE POSSIBLE IF?

▶ For thousands of years of human history, men and women stood out under the night sky, staring at the Moon and the stars, wondering what it would be like to be 'out there.'

In space. On the Moon. Beyond the earth.

On November 21, 1783, two Frenchmen made history by becoming the first people to lift off above the earth in an air balloon.

Not falling off a cliff nor jumping up high. No springs or canons.

Defying the law of gravity - they rose upward toward the heavens.

In the roughly 240 years since then, we've made incredible strides in our ability to move beyond the confines of our own orbiting world.

Sustained heavier-than-air flight with the Wright brothers. Breaking the speed of sound. Sending the first object to orbit the earth fully outside of our atmosphere. The first man in space.

And perhaps most famously, "One small step for man, One giant leap for mankind."

None of these events happened in isolation. They were, every one of them, combinations of people and breakthroughs and ideas and experiments.

At every juncture - all throughout history, from the caveman staring into space to the International Space Station still orbiting Earth today - people have asked one crucial question: "What might be possible if?"

It is an innocuous question. Full of innocence and a smidge of humility.

It has all the hallmarks of a science experiment. The adventure of a baking soda volcano. It's the shift from bottle-rockets to astrophysics.

"What might be possible if?" is a question, that when asked with enough intentionality, with enough consistency, with enough dogmatic tenacity, and hunger to find an answer, is a question that will change history.

Just ask Neil Armstrong. He walked on the moon.

ASK QUESTIONS THAT WILL CHANGE HISTORY

In the pursuit of doing things right, well-meaning managers often keep teams on a narrow path away from exploration and innovation.

After all, mistakes might be made. Time may be lost. Inconsistencies may occur.

But scale and growth and future-ready transformation do not happen by doing the same things.

What might be possible if we adjust some expectations for our team?

What might be possible if we free up some resources for innovation?

What might be possible if we give out more trust and responsibility, and freedom?

What might be possible if we take a step forward, toward our dream, just one small step?

STEP OUT
INNOVATE
TRANSFORM

START
CHANGING
THE
WORLD

TAKEOUT

Move beyond the usual ways of working. Learn to ask "What might be possible if..." questions. What might be possible if we change this element or aspect? What might be possible if we hire from outside the company? What might be possible if we add this system or process? Build "what might be possible if..." into your company culture.

CHALLENGE

What frustrates you about your current ways of working? Write down the details of the frustration. Now ask, "What might be possible if we changed this or that?" Brainstorm some new ideas. Try something new this week.

CHAPTER 28

WHAT STOPS GOOD LEADERS FROM DELEGATING MORE?

FOUR HURDLES OF DELEGATION

- Popularity
- Enthusiasm
- Cost
- Comfort

▶ Our calendar is packed. We imagine what we'd do with all those extra hours in the week if we off-loaded some tasks. What if we could just get rid of X, Y, and Z?

Off our plate and on to someone else's.

The opportunities to delegate are endless. In our minds, delegation should be easy. It's just asking someone else to get something done, right?

Yet, we all struggle to delegate. We must overcome four hurdles to truly succeed as leaders.

Hurdle 1: Comfort
"I am more comfortable doing it myself."

Our own experience – often a high level of experience – is a hurdle to successful delegation.

Why risk potentially uncomfortable change when we can happily remain in charge of the process and the outcome?

Unless we accept the challenge of the temporarily uncomfortable (as someone else learns and grows), we will forever remain behind the hurdle of what's comfortable.

We all think we're perfect at the job we do. Perhaps we are perfect.

Yet if someone can do a job 70% as well as us, we should consider delegating it out.

Learn to step out and jump the comfort hurdle.

> **If someone can do a job 70% as well as you, delegate it out.**

Hurdle 2: Cost
"It will cost too much time or money."

Yes, it might take someone an extra 3 hours to complete that task today.

Next month, however, they'll be faster, with more time spent working on more projects for more billable hours resulting in more income for our company.

Don't let short-term thinking around cost become a hurdle to delegation.

Hurdle 3: Enthusiasm
"I like this thing I do."

Sometimes, we are really, really, really passionate about what we do. We're enthusiastic.

Other times, our long-term career depends on some specific outcomes, so passion or not, we display "enthusiasm."

Yet, our high enthusiasm can be a hurdle to delegation. If we cannot let go, we cannot trust others, and then we miss an opportunity to develop and empower their growth.

Hurdle 4: Popularity
"It might not be popular."

Not every decision a leader makes is popular. Popularity is a terrible leadership motivator.

We may give away a project, only to find another team member who was really hoping to take on that same project. Someone will be disappointed.

If you're leading a team, and you delegate out part of your outcomes and responsibilities, it might be unpopular.

Perhaps whoever gains a new level of responsibility isn't as well respected. Or as well understood.

If we hold back from delegating, we miss out. Be brave enough to make a delegation decision that is right rather than what is popular.

Learn to jump the popularity hurdle.

Start with delegating one thing on your "to-do" list today. Train someone else to do it. Follow up tomorrow and the next day, and by next month it may not be on your list. Only on theirs.

Regardless of your organizational role - the newest employee or the CEO - there is always something to delegate.

Overcome the four hurdles of delegation and jump into a new season of leadership.

> **Delegate one thing on your "to-do" list today.**

TAKEOUT

Everyone faces four hurdles when delegating, whether we're giving out tasks or decision-making authority: comfort, cost, enthusiasm, and popularity. Great leaders learn to recognize and overcome these hurdles. If someone can do a job 70% as well as us, take the opportunity to delegate it out (so someone else can learn too!).

CHALLENGE

Write down two things you need to delegate this week. What hurdles influence your delegation? How are those hurdles easy/hard to overcome? Now you recognize the hurdles to overcome, when will you delegate?

29
CHAPTER

> **HOW DO YOU SET YOURSELF UP FOR SUCCESS?**

PRESPOND

(NOT A WORD, BUT ALSO NOT A TYPO)

▶ We live in a world of reactions. Hit the Like Button. Put an emoji in there. Give a thumbs up. The world demands we respond.

But within that demand, someone else is driving our attention. Someone else is pushing us forward (or sideways). Someone else is in control. And we react. We respond. We reply.

What if we changed that habit? What if, instead of waiting for the 'world' to act first, we determined to go first ourselves? What if we were the pioneer?

What if we set ourselves up for success?

As leaders, we must learn to set ourselves a presponse. A pre-response. Make a plan to prespond.

Knowing we have a difficult conversation coming up this week, what is our presponse for success?

Knowing our yearly audit is coming, what is our presponse for success?

Disclosure time: I remember going to work loaded for bear. Livid. Wild. On the edge of unruly. The whole drive, I sat there, churning the imaginary conversation over in my head. Planning what to say. Predicting the response. Arguing solo.

I don't even remember what I was mad about now. But I know that I set a presponse of how I would enter the conversation. And how I would win (I didn't).

How often do we do this at work too? Knowing we have a critical conversation ahead of us, yet dooming our outcome by setting a presponse that is hard-hitting and sharp.

What if we took a different approach? What if our presponse was to seek understanding? And to listen. To remain calm no matter how we feel.

There is a reason airline pilots say "Remain Calm" in a crisis.
It works!

So what events do you have coming up? What conversations are just around the corner that might require a clear presponse for success?

And what is that presponse that will help you, and those around you, succeed?

HOW ARE YOU SETTING YOURSELF UP FOR SUCCESS?

TAKEOUT

Make time to prespond, to plan forward for how you will speak and act (or not act). Set yourself up for success early.

CHALLENGE

What is one challenging conversation you need to have in the next two weeks? What sort of presponse do you need to set for yourself? How are you setting yourself up for success in that situation?

30
CHAPTER

> **HOW DO YOU INSPIRE PEOPLE GIVE THEIR BEST?**

CONNECT
BEYOND
VISION

▶ Someone asked me recently, "How do you inspire people to show up and produce their best - day in and day out - when you don't pay them?"

For over a decade, I worked with professional volunteers. People who paid their own way to have the privilege of being part of the projects and people we worked with.

It can be hard enough to motivate people with pay and benefits. But when those elements are not even on the table, then what? How do you get the most out of people?

Some teams I worked with drilled wells in Africa during a cease-fire from civil war. Others work through the Montana winter to build homes for those needing affordable housing. It's no small task.

It's not just young people volunteering either. I once worked with a former NASA engineer who helped launch the Saturn projects to the Moon.

I also worked with a former Ambassador. And a pro-surf photographer. There was even a 92-year-old great-grandad with a passion for teaching English. And yes, lots of young people too.

So what is it? What's the secret sauce for getting the most out of people? For creating alignment and buy-in and commitment?

- Part One is Vision.
- Part Two is Connection to that Vision.
- Part Three is Connection to People with a Connection to that Vision.

Part One: Vision

Think about your last vacation. You paid to be there: to see something, to taste it, or smell it. Or at least watch it happen. You were a part of an experience, and you wanted to be there.

Create a vision that makes people want to be there. A vision people want to grasp. And be a part of. Set a vision before people that invites participation and transformation.

Give a vision that includes them but is currently beyond them.

For example, I know a team with a vision to shift their nation from being a charity receiving nation, to a charity sending nation, in one generation. It's a big vision people want to be part of. A whole country transformed in one generation. And they're doing it too.

WHAT IS YOUR VISION THAT KEEPS PEOPLE LOOKING TO INFINITY AND BEYOND?

Part Two: Connection to that Vision

Why does someone join Greenpeace? Or any organization? Not just work for, but actively participate with a group of like-minded people - Why join?

We have to understand what is the story behind why we do what we do.

What experiences shape us? What creates connections to ideas and ideals far beyond the reach of one individual?

Connection to a vision anchors people.

Think about it: At some point, the cost of achieving any vision blurs people's ability to see that vision. So the anchoring connection becomes essential. That connection is critical to getting the most out of people (and giving the most fulfillment back to people).

Some visions create connections without trying. I imagine Greenpeace is one of them. A love for fluffy penguins as a child; the moral outrage of environmental impacts threatening those same penguins; it is a connection easily won.

However, most leaders need to listen to their staff first. And then emphasize elements of the current vision that connect to their team.

What is it about what you do - or what you could do - that connects people to the bigger picture?

Part 3: Connection to People with a Connection to that Vision

Life gets hard: pressures mount, budgets shrink, priorities rise. And sometimes people have a terrible day.

When your back is against a wall, you want to feel there's someone you know and trust and respect there beside you. Someone you're connected with. Someone also anchored to the vision you're working so hard to achieve.

And when it's time to celebrate, you want to celebrate with your friends. With people with a connection to that vision.

So what is your vision? And how well does your team know it?

How can you help connect them to that vision? And to each other, so they're well-positioned to thrive together no matter what comes?

TAKEOUT

Getting the best out of people (and giving the best to people) requires connecting people to other people with a connection to a vision. When people see their hard work directly impacting the people around them and reaching visionary goals, they give extra effort.

CHALLENGE

Write a list of five people you're connected to who are also connected to your vision. How strong is that connection? What can you do to build a stronger connection this week?

WHAT QUESTION DO I NEED TO ANSWER THIS WEEK?

WHERE TO FROM HERE?

What is most important and relevant for you today?

Think about your world, work, home life, and who you are as a leader. Which chapter(s) do you need to go back and read again? Which challenge(s) do you need to apply? What might be possible if you apply a good leadership book for yourself?

Then, begin to implement it with your team. Discuss it together. Apply it together. Reframe your circumstances and approach your leadership journey from a new perspective.

Finally, practice this book within your community. What elements of clarity, culture, and communication need evaluating? Question best practice. Look at what might be possible. Know your ranch and connect beyond vision. Impact the opportunities you see.

To explore the ideas in *A Good Leadership Book* in greater detail, or to explore individual or team coaching, reach Dan at www.leadcoachrelease.com.

MUST READ BOOKS

Atomic Habits
| James Clear

Building a StoryBrand
| Donald Miller

Essentialism
| Greg McKeown

Originals
| Adam Grant

QBQ! The Question Behind the Question
| John G. Miller

Radical Candor
| Kim Scott

Rework
| Jason Fried & David Hansson

Silos, Politics, and Turf Wars
| Patrick Lencioni

The Infinite Game
| Simon Sinek

The Power of Full Engagement
| Jim Loehr & Tony Schwartz

This is Marketing
| Seth Godin

To Sell is Human
| Dan Pink

Turn the Ship Around!
| L. David Marquet

ABOUT THE AUTHOR

Dan Lake has explored good leadership on five continents. His interest in clarity, culture, and communication began when he was a bungy jump instructor and tour guide. A career highlight is the months he spent living in India teaching English to Tibetan monks. His favorite question is, "How can I help you succeed?"

As a manager and coach in one of the world's largest not-for-profit organizations, he capitalized on multi-national opportunities to help emerging leaders lift and shift their leadership potential. As a founder and director, Dan turns possibilities and options into meaningful work, systems, and friendships with a lasting global impact.

Dan is a trusted advisor, speaker, and mentor. He has extensive experience with emerging leaders and senior management teams covering operations, training, coaching, and development. Some of those leaders serve organizations such as the US State Department, Tesla, Google, and Apple.

Dan holds a master's degree in leadership, where he focused his thesis work on the Millennial generation. He hopes this book helps serve your success as a leader.

Printed in Poland
by Amazon Fulfillment
Poland Sp. z o.o., Wrocław

31736099R00128